INSIDE THE NFL

CLEVELAND BROWNS

by Charlie Beattie

Abdo & Daughters
MIDDLE GRADE NONFICTION

An imprint of Abdo Publishing
abdobooks.com

ABDOBOOKS.COM

Published by Abdo Publishing, a division of ABDO, PO Box 398166, Minneapolis, Minnesota 55439.

Printed in China.
052025
092025

THIS BOOK CONTAINS RECYCLED MATERIALS

Cover Photos: Nick Cammett/Diamond Images/Getty Images (Myles Garrett); Focus on Sport/Getty Images (Jim Brown)
Interior Photos: Nick Cammett/Diamond Images/Getty Images, 4–5, 6, 55; Nick Cammett/Getty Images Sport/Getty Images, 7, 59; Frank Jansky/Icon Sportswire/Getty Images, 8, 61 (bottom right); Aaron Doster/AP Images, 9, 63; Abdo Publishing, 10–11; Bettmann/Getty Images, 12–13, 16, 17, 18, 26, 60 (bottom left); Julian C. Wilson/AP Images, 14; AP Images, 15, 19, 22–23, 28, 29; Vic Stein/Getty Images Sport/Getty Images, 20; Harold P. Matosian/AP Images, 21, 60 (top); Focus on Sport/Getty Images, 24, 30, 32, 34–35, 38, 60 (bottom middle); Robert Riger/Getty Images Sport/Getty Images, 25; Focus on Sport/Getty Images Sport/Getty Images, 27, 37 (bottom), 60 (bottom right); James Drake/Getty Images Sport/Getty Images, 31, 33; George Gojkovich/Getty Images Sport/Getty Images, 36, 37 (top), 40, 50, 61 (top left); Paul Spinelli/NFL Photos/AP Images, 39, 43; Mark Duncan/AP Images, 41, 42, 44–45; Rick Stewart/Getty Images Sport/Getty Images, 46–47; Stephen Dunn/Getty Images Sport/Getty Images, 48; Tony Dejak/AP Images, 49, 61 (bottom left); Scott Boehm/AP Images, 52; Paul Spinelli/AP Images, 53, 61 (top right); Winslow Townson/AP Images, 54; David Eulitt/Getty Images Sport/Getty Images, 56; David Richard/AP Images, 57; Shutterstock Images, 58

Editor: Haley Williams
Series Designer: Laura Graphenteen
Production Designer: Katharine Hale

Library of Congress Control Number: 2024948492

Publisher's Cataloging-in-Publication Data

Names: Beattie, Charlie, author.
Title: Cleveland Browns / by Charlie Beattie
Description: Minneapolis, Minnesota: Abdo Publishing, 2026 | Series: Inside the NFL | Includes online resources and index.
Identifiers: ISBN 9781098296698 (lib. bdg.) | ISBN 9798384919216 (ebook)
Subjects: LCSH: Cleveland Browns (Football team: 1999-)--Juvenile literature. | National Football League--Juvenile literature. | Football teams--Juvenile literature. | American football--Juvenile literature.
Classification: DDC 796.33264--dc23

CONTENTS

Cleveland Browns defensive end Myles Garrett, *right*, chases after Tennessee Titans quarterback Ryan Tannehill during a 2023 game.

CHAPTER 1

SACK MASTER

Cleveland Browns defensive end Myles Garrett dug his right hand into the ground and awaited the snap. He knew the Tennessee Titans would be passing the ball. That meant Garrett had one job. He needed to get to Tennessee quarterback Ryan Tannehill.

The Browns' defense was backed up near its own goal line. Cleveland had a 13–3 lead with 13 seconds left in the first half of the Week 3 National Football League (NFL) game on September 24, 2023. Garrett was poised to pounce at the snap of the ball. He wanted to maintain Cleveland's advantage.

THE TOP CHOICE

Just a few years earlier, the Browns finished the 2016 season with the league's worst record at 1–15. The following spring, they had the No. 1

Garrett, *right*, poses with his father after the Browns took the defensive end with the top pick in the 2017 NFL Draft.

pick in the 2017 NFL Draft. The Browns needed help at all positions, but one player stood out.

Garrett completed his junior season at Texas A&M in 2016. The defensive end was one of college football's most dominant players. Although he suffered through a few injuries during the season, he still finished with 8 1/2 sacks. At 6 feet, 4 inches, and 272 pounds with long, muscular arms, Garrett could plow through opposing offensive tackles. He also had great speed, allowing him to simply blaze past blockers. With such an array of skills, the 21-year-old was considered the draft's top pick. One scout joked that if the Browns didn't take Garrett, the team should be kicked out of the NFL.

Cleveland did take Garrett, although he wasn't much help right away. The Browns were even worse in his rookie season in 2017, finishing with an 0–16 record. But Garrett picked up seven sacks in 11 games and looked to be a potential star. The next year, he had 13 1/2 sacks and was named to the Pro Bowl. Slowly, Cleveland started to add more talent around Garrett.

As the 2023 season opened, the Browns had high hopes. They had one of the best defenses in the NFL, with Garrett at the heart of things. He was coming off five straight seasons of double-digit sack totals, and he wanted to get the new year off to a good start.

TAKEDOWNS

Late in the first quarter against the Titans, Garrett made his first big impact. Tennessee faced second-and-13 at the Browns' 20. On the snap, Garrett burst forward. He drove into Titans lineman Andre Dillard, shoving him back toward Tannehill. Although Dillard tried to

Garrett, *left*, had at least one sack in nine of the 16 games he played in 2023.

Garrett, *center*, celebrates his second-quarter sack with teammates Ogbo Okoronkwo, *left*, and Dalvin Tomlinson.

get in the way, Garrett pushed all the way to the quarterback. While Dillard hung on, Garrett reached out his right arm and swatted the ball loose for a fumble. The Titans recovered and kicked a field goal. But it was an early sign of what Garrett would do that game.

In the second quarter, with the Browns up 10–3, the Titans were driving. On third-and-11 from the Cleveland 40, Garrett and fellow defensive end Ogbo Okoronkwo swooped in and buried Tannehill together. The Titans were forced to punt, and Cleveland added a field goal on its next drive.

Tennessee put together another drive to get to the Browns' 11-yard line with 13 seconds left in the second quarter. The Titans had no timeouts, but they wanted to try a quick pass for a score before going for a field goal. Garrett, however, had other plans.

Lined up wide of Dillard, Garrett exploded forward at the snap. Dillard made contact, trying to slow down Garrett. But the Browns' star bulldozed his way forward, taking the huge tackle with him straight into Tannehill. Garrett dropped the quarterback at the 23-yard line, ending the half.

The Titans' deficit had grown to 20–3 when they faced third-and-12 from their own 8-yard line early in the fourth quarter. Once again, Garrett burst past Dillard, using his left arm to fend off the Titans' tackle. Garrett wrapped up Tannehill at the goal line. Tannehill managed to slip away, but Garrett recovered to bring the quarterback down at the 3-yard line.

The play ended another Titans drive, and it gave Garrett 3 1/2 sacks on the day. The Browns rolled to a 27–3 victory. Cleveland fans had witnessed the many highs and lows of the team for decades. Garrett's big game was just the latest incredible moment in the Browns' colorful and storied history.

PERSONAL BEST

Myles Garrett's game against Tennessee was impressive. But it wasn't the best statistical performance of his career. On September 26, 2021, Garrett piled up a Cleveland-record 4 1/2 sacks in a game against the Chicago Bears. At one point in the second quarter, Garrett took down Bears quarterback Justin Fields on back-to-back plays.

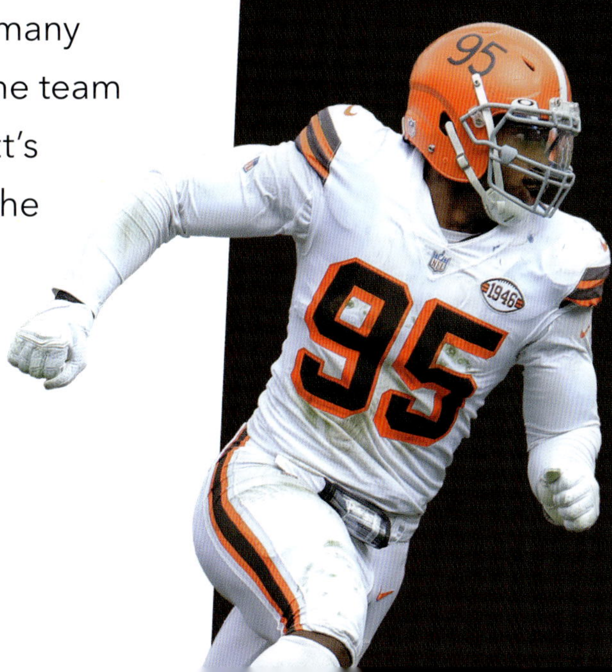

Garrett finished both the 2021 and 2022 seasons with 16 sacks.

NFL TEAMS MAP

NFC

NFC EAST

- DALLAS COWBOYS
- NEW YORK GIANTS
- PHILADELPHIA EAGLES
- WASHINGTON COMMANDERS

NFC WEST

- ARIZONA CARDINALS
- LOS ANGELES RAMS
- SAN FRANCISCO 49ERS
- SEATTLE SEAHAWKS

NFC NORTH

- CHICAGO BEARS
- DETROIT LIONS
- GREEN BAY PACKERS
- MINNESOTA VIKINGS

NFC SOUTH

- ATLANTA FALCONS
- CAROLINA PANTHERS
- NEW ORLEANS SAINTS
- TAMPA BAY BUCCANEERS

AFC

AFC EAST	AFC WEST	AFC NORTH	AFC SOUTH
BUFFALO BILLS	DENVER BRONCOS	BALTIMORE RAVENS	HOUSTON TEXANS
MIAMI DOLPHINS	KANSAS CITY CHIEFS	CINCINNATI BENGALS	INDIANAPOLIS COLTS
NEW ENGLAND PATRIOTS	LAS VEGAS RAIDERS	CLEVELAND BROWNS	JACKSONVILLE JAGUARS
NEW YORK JETS	LOS ANGELES CHARGERS	PITTSBURGH STEELERS	TENNESSEE TITANS

Quarterback Otto Graham, *left*, throws a pass during a game between the Browns and the New York Yankees in 1948.

CHAPTER 2

PAUL'S TEAM

OHIO HAS LONG BEEN A RENOWNED FOOTBALL STATE. THE LEAGUE NOW known as the NFL formed in 1920 in the city of Canton in northeast Ohio. Five of the league's original 14 teams played in the state. Although the NFL had shrunk by 1945, the Cleveland Rams professional football team still represented the biggest city in Ohio. But after winning that year's championship, the Rams packed up and left for Los Angeles.

Cleveland didn't have to wait long for a new team. However, the Rams' replacement would not play in the NFL. A year before the Rams left, Chicago sportswriter Arch Ward founded a new league called the All-America Football Conference (AAFC). The AAFC opened play in 1946 with eight teams, including a new Cleveland franchise.

Paul Brown, *center*, was enlisted in the US Navy when Mickey McBride, *left*, hired him to coach Cleveland.

INSTANT DYNASTY

The new Cleveland team was owned by local businessman Arthur "Mickey" McBride. In targeting a head coach, he stayed close to home. Paul Brown had been a legendary high school coach at the storied Massillon High School, 54 miles (87 km) south of Cleveland. He had also coached Ohio State to its first national championship in 1942. McBride hired Brown in 1946 as coach and general manager, and he also gave Brown part ownership of the team. The two then asked fans to vote on a team nickname. The head coach was so popular that the winning vote was cast for "Browns." Brown didn't like the choice, but he eventually went along with it.

The Browns' nickname was just one small piece of Paul Brown's football legacy. The forward-thinking coach is credited with inventing football staples such as the face mask, draw play, and modern playbook. In addition to those creations, Brown had an eye for talent. Many of his first stars were players who had been in the military. Some had seen heavy fighting in World War II (1939–1945). Compared to war, they thought Brown's tough practices and the on-field struggles of football were a breeze.

One of Brown's first signings was versatile quarterback Otto Graham. Brown also recruited stars such as receivers Dante Lavelli and Mac Speedie, center Frank Gatski, and defensive player Tom Colella. Kicker Lou "the Toe" Groza was such a weapon that he changed how other teams looked at kickers. The field goal was an

Mac Speedie was the AAFC's leading receiver every year from 1947 to 1949.

RADIO SIGNALS

Another idea by Paul Brown was a radio headset fixed inside his quarterback's helmet. That way, Brown could verbally send plays in from the sideline. The NFL quickly banned the idea, but it proved to be ahead of its time. Today, all NFL quarterback helmets are wired to communicate with the team's coaching staff. Each team also has one designated defensive player who can do the same.

afterthought in the NFL's early days, as few players could kick accurately. Groza's consistent play meant the Browns could count on three points if their offense was stopped within his range.

Two of Brown's biggest early signings came as the result of the coach's progressive attitude toward race. In the 1940s, America's top sports leagues were segregated. When Brown signed hulking fullback Marion Motley and small but speedy defensive lineman Bill Willis, the two Black players helped break the color barrier in professional football. Although frequently discriminated against on the road and on the field, both Motley and Willis were stars for Cleveland.

With a core group of excellent players in place, the Browns debuted on September 6, 1946, with a 44–0 demolition of the Miami Seahawks. More than 60,000 fans attended the game at Cleveland Municipal Stadium. It was a sign of things to come. Cleveland started

Fullback Marion Motley rushed for 4,720 yards and 31 touchdowns during his nine-year pro career.

7-0 that season, allowing only 34 points in the process before finishing with a 12-2 record. In the league's first championship game, Graham's fourth-quarter touchdown pass to Lavelli secured a 14-9 win for the Browns over the New York Yankees.

Over the next three seasons, Cleveland lost only two games. The dominant Browns' best year was 1948, when they finished 14-0 and outscored their opponents by almost 200 points. It was the first time a professional football team had ever gone undefeated and untied over an entire season.

Cleveland players celebrate with coach Paul Brown, *center*, after winning their fourth straight AAFC title game in 1949.

SWITCHING LEAGUES

The Browns were such a powerhouse that other AAFC teams couldn't keep up. Fans in other cities started giving up on their teams. With attendance flagging, the league began to fail. The AAFC ceased operations after the 1949 season, but the Browns lived on. They were one of three teams absorbed into the NFL in time for the 1950 season.

Few people thought the Browns could continue their championship streak in the NFL. The AAFC was thought to be a far weaker league. "The worst team in our league could beat the best team in theirs," one NFL owner said.

As if to drive home the point, the NFL scheduled Cleveland to debut on the road against the defending champion, the Philadelphia Eagles. Instead of being humiliated, the Browns shocked everyone with a 35–10 rout. Graham carved up the Eagles' powerful defense with 346 passing yards and three touchdowns. "They didn't upset us," Eagles tackle Bucko Kilroy said. "Man for man, they were just a better team."

"THEY DIDN'T UPSET US. MAN FOR MAN, THEY WERE JUST A BETTER TEAM."

—BUCKO KILROY

The Browns ended up going 10–2 that season. Motley led the NFL with 810 rushing yards, and halfback Dub Jones scored 11 total touchdowns. Cleveland beat the New York Giants in a one-game playoff to reach the NFL title game against Cleveland's old team, the Los Angeles Rams.

Halfback Dub Jones (40) tied an NFL record by scoring six touchdowns during a 1951 game against the Chicago Bears.

Graham was so nervous before games that he could barely eat. But once on the field, he was so

Kicker Lou Groza, *center,* holds up the shoe he used to kick the game-winning field goal in the 1950 NFL Championship Game.

consistent that he earned the nickname "Automatic Otto." He always seemed to step up when the Browns needed him most.

The Browns entered the fourth quarter trailing Los Angeles 28–20. With under 10 minutes left, Graham led Cleveland on a long drive in which the Browns converted three fourth downs. From the Rams' 14-yard line, Graham threw the ball to the corner of the end zone, where receiver Rex Bumgardner made a diving catch. It was Graham's fourth touchdown pass of the game. Groza's extra point cut the Rams' lead to one point.

The Browns got the ball back with 1:48 left. Graham drove the team down the field with a 16-yard run and four complete passes. In the final seconds, Groza knocked through a 16-yard field goal to put the Browns ahead 30–28. Cleveland's defense sealed the win with an interception on the Rams' next drive. After time ran out, fans at Cleveland Municipal Stadium stormed the field in celebration.

A SECOND TITLE

The championship debut established the Browns as a force in their new league. But winning again proved to be tricky. In 1951, they played the Rams for the title for the second straight season. This time, Los Angeles won 24–17 on a late touchdown pass. In both 1952 and 1953, the Browns reached the championship game only to lose to the Detroit Lions.

Before the 1954 season, both Motley and Willis retired. Graham also announced that he would play only one more season. He had to shoulder even more of the offensive load. It didn't seem to bother him, though. Graham threw 11 touchdown passes and rushed for a team-high eight scores. After a 9–3 season, the Browns squared off with Detroit again in the NFL Championship Game.

The 1952 and 1953 games had been close. In 1954, Graham made sure Cleveland didn't fall again. He threw two touchdown passes in the first quarter to help build a 14–3 lead. He then added two rushing touchdowns and his third touchdown pass in the second. At halftime, Cleveland led 35–10. By the time Graham plunged in from 1 yard out in the third quarter, the game was effectively over.

The final score was 56–10. That win would have been a fitting end to Graham's career. However, Brown was not ready to let him go. After struggling to find a replacement quarterback in training camp before the 1955

Graham played in either the AAFC or the NFL title game every season of his 10-year career.

Graham (14) scores the final touchdown of his career in the 1955 NFL Championship Game against the Los Angeles Rams.

season, Brown offered Graham a then-record $25,000 to come back for one more year.

With Graham tossing 15 touchdown passes and rushing for six scores, the 1955 Browns once again reached the NFL title game. There, they faced the Rams for a third time. Playing on the road in Los Angeles, Graham threw two touchdowns and rushed for two more. The Browns' defense also snagged seven interceptions in the team's 38–14 win.

With the outcome all but decided in the fourth quarter, Brown removed Graham from the game. As the quarterback walked off the field, the opposing fans gave him a standing ovation. In his time with the team, Graham won 105 games and lost only 17, with four ties. No quarterback has won a higher percentage of his games since. Graham left behind a legacy that was nearly impossible to repeat.

Before joining the Browns, fullback Jim Brown was a star lacrosse, track and field, and football player at Syracuse.

CHAPTER 3

THE LAST CHAMPIONS

IN 1956, THE BROWNS EXPERIENCED A LOSING RECORD FOR THE FIRST time in their 11 seasons as a team. But there was one positive that came out of it. After finishing 5–7, the Browns had the sixth pick in the 1957 NFL Draft.

Paul Brown hoped to grab a new quarterback with this pick. But when the top signal-callers were taken, he drafted running back Jim Brown instead. Beyond having the perfect name to play in Cleveland, Jim Brown was built to dominate in the NFL. Standing 6 feet, 2 inches tall, and weighing 232 pounds, he was the size of most linemen at that time.

The five players picked ahead of Brown all became stars. Two of them went on to have Hall of Fame careers. However, when football experts discuss the greatest player of all time, Brown is always at or near the top of the list.

When he wasn't bowling over defenders, Brown had the speed to blow past them. With his combination of size and speed, he was terrifying to play against, and even tougher to bring down. The running back also had a particular trick. As a player wrapped him up, Brown would make his legs go slightly limp. When the defender then eased up, thinking he had the running back down, Brown would surge forward and break free.

Jim Brown was named to the All-Pro team eight times in his nine NFL seasons.

Brown led the NFL in rushing as a rookie, gaining 942 yards and scoring a league-high 10 touchdowns. He became the first player to ever win Rookie of the Year and Most Valuable Player (MVP) in the same season. His performance also helped Cleveland get back to the title game, but the Browns were blown away by the rival Detroit Lions 59–14. The new star's second year was even better. Brown rushed for 1,527 yards, 400 more than the old NFL record. He also led the league with 18 total touchdowns. "[Jim Brown] was the best running back I've ever seen in my life or played against in my life," said Hall of Fame safety Paul Krause.

"[JIM BROWN] WAS THE BEST RUNNING BACK I'VE EVER SEEN IN MY LIFE OR PLAYED AGAINST IN MY LIFE."

—PAUL KRAUSE

BATTLE OF THE BROWNS

Despite Jim Brown's greatness, Cleveland struggled to get back to its early glory days. The Browns got off to a strong start in 1958 and went into the final week of the season with a one-game lead over the New York Giants. However, the Giants beat the Browns 13–10 to force a first-place tie, and then they shut down Cleveland again the next week in the playoffs. With a spot in the NFL Championship Game on the line, New York held Brown to just 8 yards in a 10–0 loss for Cleveland.

Quarterback Milt Plum (16) is sacked by three New York Giants defenders.

Art Modell, *left*, paid $4 million to buy the Cleveland Browns in 1961.

Harnessing Jim Brown wasn't easy. And no one found it more difficult than Paul Brown. The running back was as strongheaded as his head coach, and the two did not always see eye to eye on what was best for the team. Jim Brown thought the coach was too controlling, especially with the team's quarterbacks. At the time, most quarterbacks called plays on the field. Paul Brown insisted the team should run what he chose on each down. The coach sometimes struggled with Jim Brown's attitude. At halftime of a game in 1959, Paul Brown even accused Jim Brown of faking an injury.

In 1961, advertising executive Art Modell bought the Browns. Modell made a quick friendship with the team's running back. But he constantly battled the head coach. Paul Brown had always had control over Cleveland's roster. When he made trades without telling the new owner, Modell was furious. It didn't help that the team was falling short of the title game, even with Jim Brown's greatness leading Cleveland to winning seasons in the early 1960s. After the Browns finished 7-6-1 in 1962 and missed the playoffs for the fourth year in a row, Modell fired Paul Brown.

The move shocked football fans. No coach and team were more closely connected than Paul Brown and Cleveland. Pete Rozelle, the NFL commissioner at the time, tried to talk Modell out of the move. But the new owner stuck to his decision.

PAUL BROWN'S REVENGE

Paul Brown never got over his firing in Cleveland. However, in 1967, he founded a new team in the American Football League (AFL). The Cincinnati Bengals wore orange and brown uniforms, just like the Browns. When the AFL and NFL merged in 1970, the Browns and Bengals began a fierce rivalry. In addition to owning the team, Brown was also its first head coach. Today, Brown's family still owns the Bengals.

Paul Brown coached the Bengals from 1968 to 1975.

BACK ON TOP

In Paul Brown's place, Modell promoted assistant coach Blanton Collier. Collier allowed his players more freedom than Paul Brown did. Under the new coach, Jim Brown became a threat in both the passing and running game. During the 1964 season, quarterback

Wide receiver Paul Warfield caught 271 passes, including 52 touchdowns, in eight seasons with the Browns.

Frank Ryan had a pair of excellent receivers in rookie Paul Warfield and veteran Gary Collins to throw to.

The Browns averaged nearly 30 points per game while finishing 10–3–1 in 1964, earning the team a spot in the title game against the Baltimore Colts. Collins spent the week leading up to the game predicting a Cleveland victory. He also wanted the game's MVP Award, and the brand-new sports car that came with it.

No receiver had ever been the MVP of a championship game in the NFL before. It didn't look likely for Collins after a scoreless first half on a windy day in Cleveland. But Ryan and Collins came alive after halftime. After Lou Groza made a field goal, Ryan hit Collins on an 18-yard touchdown pass. Later in the third quarter, Ryan and Collins hooked up again for a 42-yard touchdown. Finally, they put the game away with a 51-yard connection in the fourth. The Browns won 27–0, and Collins got his car after being named MVP.

Quarterback Frank Ryan waves to the camera in the locker room after Cleveland beat the Baltimore Colts in the 1964 NFL title game.

WALKING AWAY

Jim Brown was just 29 years old when he retired from the NFL.

In 1965, Jim Brown led the NFL in rushing for the eighth time in nine seasons. He also had a career high 21 touchdowns, 17 of those rushing, and won the league's MVP for the third time. Cleveland reached the championship game again but lost 23–12 to the Green Bay Packers, whose tough defense held Brown to just 50 yards.

That game turned out to be Brown's last. By the mid-1960s he was also acting in movies. In addition, Brown was passionate about political causes and became a civil rights activist. He retired in 1966 to focus on his new passions.

The legacy Jim Brown left behind was unmatched. His 12,312 rushing yards and 106 rushing touchdowns were both NFL records at the time he retired. Six decades after his retirement, Brown's 10 games with at least three rushing scores was still a league record. However, his impact on professional football went far beyond his numbers. Since the day he retired, every successful NFL running back has been measured against the standards Brown set.

Lou Groza (76) scored 1,608 points in his professional football career.

NEW STARS

In 1966, the Browns celebrated their 20th season. It had been two decades filled with some of the greatest names in football. But only one of the team's original stars was still left.

Groza started his career as both a kicker and offensive lineman. He retired after the 1959 season but was lured back in 1961 as just a kicker. In 1966, Groza was 42 years old and already the league's all-time leading scorer. He played two final seasons but struggled, hitting only 20 of 46 field-goal attempts. When Groza retired in 1967, the last link to the original Browns was gone.

Despite the new faces, the team was still winning games. Collier promoted Jim Brown's backup, Leroy Kelly, as the new starting running back. Kelly soon became a star, leading the league in rushing yards in both 1967 and 1968. Unlike Brown, who often ran over opposing defenders, Kelly relied on his quick moves to dance around would-be tacklers.

Running back Leroy Kelly looks for an opening in a 1967 game against the Dallas Cowboys.

The Browns reached back-to-back NFL title games in 1968 and 1969. This time, there was a new prize to play for. In 1966, the NFL and rival American Football League (AFL) agreed to have their champions meet in a game now known as Super Bowl I. The Browns met the Baltimore Colts in the 1968 playoffs to fight for the NFL's spot in Super Bowl III. However, Baltimore shut out the Browns 34–0. The following season, the Browns lost the NFL title game to the Minnesota Vikings 27–7. Only a late touchdown pass from quarterback Bill Nelson to Collins prevented another shutout. More than 50 years later, the Browns were still trying to reach their first Super Bowl.

The Browns battle the Minnesota Vikings in the NFL Championship Game after the 1969 season.

In 1970, the NFL and AFL merged. To balance the leagues, three NFL teams joined the AFL teams to create the American Football Conference (AFC). The Browns were one of those teams. For two decades, Cleveland had been one of the faces of the NFL. But as the team moved into a new era, everything was about to change.

Quarterback Mike Phipps threw five interceptions in the 1972 divisional playoff game against the Miami Dolphins.

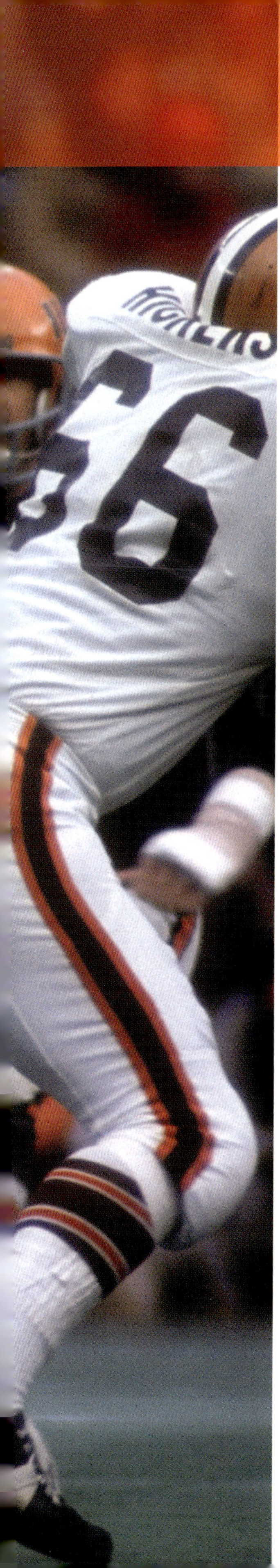

CHAPTER 4

END OF AN ERA

BLANTON COLLIER STEPPED OUT OF PAUL BROWN'S MASSIVE SHADOW to become a respected head coach. However, by the late 1960s, he was losing his hearing. During the 1970 season, the 64-year-old Collier struggled to communicate with players on the field, and he often couldn't hear interview questions from reporters. So after a 7–7 finish that year, Collier retired. Offensive coordinator Nick Skorich took over as just the third head coach in Cleveland's history.

Two years later, the Browns entered the 1972 playoffs against the heavily favored Miami Dolphins. The Browns were strong with a 10–4 record. However, the 14–0 Dolphins were seeking to become the first perfect champions in NFL history. After falling behind 10–0, Cleveland rallied in the second half. With 8:11 left in the

The Browns had only one winning season between 1974 and 1977.

game, quarterback Mike Phipps tossed a 27-yard touchdown pass to receiver Fair Hooker to put the Browns up 14–13. But Miami responded with a long drive that ended in an 8-yard touchdown run, which the Browns couldn't answer. Phipps threw an interception in the final minute to seal the loss.

The season proved to be the last high point in the 1970s for the Browns. In 1974, Skorich oversaw just the second losing record in team history. Within three years, that total had doubled.

RIVERBOAT SAM

Before the 1978 season, Cleveland brought in another new head coach. Sam Rutigliano favored high-powered offensive football. Rutigliano often took risks other coaches would not. That gambling mentality earned him the nickname "Riverboat Sam."

Rutigliano's aerial attack turned struggling quarterback Brian Sipe into one of the league's best passers. In 1980, Sipe was named the NFL MVP after throwing for 4,132 yards and 30 touchdowns. He was joined by a strong cast of receivers such as Reggie Rucker, Dave Logan, and the pass-catching backfield duo of Greg Pruitt and Mike Pruitt, who were not related. The team became known as "the Kardiac Kids" after winning several close games that year.

Running back Mike Pruitt had 6,540 career rushing yards with the Browns.

One of Sipe's favorite targets, though, was tight end Ozzie Newsome. In 1978, "the Wizard of Oz" had been one of two first-round draft picks for the Browns. The other was linebacker

Tight end Ozzie Newsome caught a team-record 662 passes in his career.

Clay Matthews. Both players went on to have careers that rank among the best in team history. Matthews was a ferocious hitter, and Newsome helped change the way tight ends played. In the NFL's early days, tight ends were thought of merely as extra linemen. Newsome could certainly block, but the future Hall of Famer was also a swift runner with excellent hands.

RED RIGHT 88

The Browns finished 11–5 in 1980 to earn their first division title in nine years. In the divisional round of the playoffs, Cleveland hosted the Oakland Raiders. Playing in temperatures that hovered around 0 degrees Fahrenheit (–18°C), both teams struggled offensively. The Browns led for much of the day but fell behind 14–12 early in the fourth quarter. That was still the score in the final minutes as the Browns got the ball and drove down the field.

Cleveland faced second-and-nine at the Raiders' 13-yard line with 49 seconds to go. The Browns needed just a field goal to take the lead. However, Rutigliano stayed true to his nickname. He sent in a passing play designated as "Red Right 88" in the Browns' playbook. Sipe's instructions, according to his coach, were to look for an open receiver. If he didn't find one, Rutigliano instructed Sipe to "throw the ball into Lake Erie," which was just outside the walls of Municipal Stadium.

Quarterback Brian Sipe broke Otto Graham's team record for passing yards in 1983.

Sipe spotted Newsome in the end zone and fired a pass to the receiver. At the last second, Oakland defensive back Mike Davis cut in front of Newsome and intercepted the pass. Red Right 88 became one of the most infamous plays in Browns history. Years later, Rutigliano said about the play, "I'd make the same call again if I was in the same position."

"I'D MAKE THE SAME CALL AGAIN IF I WAS IN THE SAME POSITION."

—SAM RUTIGLIANO

Rutigliano's Browns never got that far in the playoffs again. Cleveland reached the playoffs in 1982 but lost in the wild-card round. Two years later, Rutigliano was fired partway through the 5-11 season.

A Browns fan chews on a toy bone during a home game in 1988.

THE DAWG POUND

In training camp before the 1985 season, Browns defenders began to celebrate good plays by barking. Cornerbacks Hanford Dixon and Frank Minnifield had named the unit "dogs." Soon after, the barking spread to the stands. By the start of the season, fans were showing up to Browns

Cornerbacks Hanford Dixon, *left*, and Frank Minnifield, *right*, combined for 46 interceptions during their careers with the Browns.

games wearing dog outfits and masks. The tradition only grew from there.

"The Dawg Pound" soon became one of the most well-known cheering sections in the NFL. And the rowdy fans had plenty to cheer about in the mid-1980s. New coach Marty Schottenheimer had the Browns contending again. Matthews led the defense, while new quarterback Bernie Kosar was developing into a star. A native of Boardman, Ohio, which is just 81 miles (130 km) southeast of Cleveland, Kosar was also a fan favorite. At a time when few players wanted to come to Cleveland, Kosar publicly stated that he wanted to play for the Browns.

By 1986, Kosar was spreading the ball around to Newsome, young receivers Webster Slaughter and Brian Brennan, and the backfield duo of Earnest Byner and Kevin Mack. Cleveland went 12–4 that season. The team finally ended its 17-year playoff losing streak by beating the New York Jets 23–20 in double-overtime in the divisional round.

Cleveland hosted the Denver Broncos in the AFC title game. With just over five minutes to play, Kosar connected with Brennan on a 48-yard touchdown pass to put the Browns up 20–13. After a mistake on the kickoff return pinned the Broncos at their own 2-yard line, Cleveland's fans roared in anticipation of a possible Super Bowl appearance.

Instead, as time wound down, Denver's future Hall of Fame quarterback John Elway put together a masterful march down the field. In 15 plays, Denver went 98 yards, tying the game on a 5-yard touchdown pass with 37 seconds left. Elway's heroics went down in NFL history as "the Drive." Denver won the game 23–20 in overtime.

Browns defenders lay a big hit on a Denver Broncos runner during the AFC title game on January 11, 1987.

THE FUMBLE

A year later, the two teams met again in the AFC title game, this time in Denver. After a rough first half, Cleveland trailed 21–3. Then the Browns turned it on. By the start of the fourth quarter, Denver's lead was trimmed to 31–24. Cleveland's hero was Byner, who had a touchdown catch and touchdown run in the third quarter.

The teams traded touchdowns in the fourth. Cleveland took over late in the game down 38–31 and drove down the field. Kosar had the team in position at the Denver 8-yard line with just over a minute left. On the next play, Byner took a handoff and rushed left. The only player in his path was Broncos cornerback Jeremiah Castille. As Byner juked by, Castille threw out his left arm, stripped the ball, and recovered it. The Broncos took an intentional safety on their final

Running back Earnest Byner, *center*, has the ball stripped from his arms by Denver's Jeremiah Castille, *right*, in the AFC Championship Game in January 1988.

play, and Cleveland lost 38–33. One year after "the Drive," Byner's mistake became known as "the Fumble."

Cleveland never recovered from the two playoff disasters against Denver. The teams met again in the AFC title game after the 1989 season. But the Broncos defeated the Browns 37–21.

After missing the playoffs in 1990, Cleveland hired Bill Belichick to try and turn things around. Belichick would eventually lead the New England Patriots to six Super Bowl titles in the 2000s. But as a first-time head coach, he struggled to keep Browns fans on his side. By 1993, Kosar had battled through several injuries. Even though Kosar was no longer a star, Belichick drew the wrath of fans when he cut the veteran quarterback halfway through the season. Some die-hard Browns supporters protested at the team's practice facility.

Belichick led the team to the playoffs a year later. But it didn't matter. Browns fans were no longer worried about having a good team. By that point, they were in a fight to keep the team in town.

KOSAR'S STREAK

Quarterback Bernie Kosar reached just one Pro Bowl in his injury-riddled career. But he managed to set an impressive record in 1991. Kosar threw 308 consecutive passes without an interception. That stood as an NFL record until it was broken by Aaron Rodgers of the Green Bay Packers in 2018.

Bernie Kosar threw 116 touchdown passes in his nine seasons with the Browns.

Municipal Stadium was home to both football and baseball in Cleveland.

CHAPTER 5

THE NEW BROWNS

By 1995, Art Modell was one of the longest-standing NFL owners. He was never one of the most well-off, though. While most owners also run other businesses in addition to their football teams, Modell did not. When he bought the Browns in 1961, he left his job in advertising. The team was his only way to make money.

In the 1970s, Modell took over the Browns' stadium. Since Cleveland's baseball team also played there, Modell made money all year from Municipal Stadium. By the 1990s, however, the baseball team was moving into its own building. Municipal Stadium, which was built in 1931, was outdated and crumbling. Modell needed a brand-new home for the Browns, but the city refused to help him pay for it.

As the 1995 season unfolded, Browns fans watched helplessly as it looked as if Modell was going to move the team. The news became official on November 6 of that year. Modell held a press conference in Baltimore saying he would move the Browns there, since the city had lost the Colts to Indianapolis in 1984. The reaction in Cleveland was fierce. Fans protested. Some even threatened Modell's life. The owner-turned-enemy never returned to Cleveland.

Fans spent the final seven weeks of the season grieving the loss of their iconic team. Although the Browns had mostly struggled

The news of the Browns' move was devastating to many fans.

on the field for the previous 25 years, the connection to the team's glory years had never faded. The final home game in Cleveland was on December 17, 1995. Upset fans disrupted the win over the Cincinnati Bengals by throwing items on the field. The Dawg Pound, behind one end zone, was particularly bad. Devoted fans ripped out entire rows of seats and tossed them onto the field.

City officials tried to sue Modell to keep the team. Eventually, the league worked out a solution. Cleveland could keep the Browns' nickname and history. But the players and staff would start a new

Fans throw stadium seats onto the field during the Browns' last home game of the 1995 season.

life as the Baltimore Ravens. The NFL also promised a new team in Cleveland by 1999 if the city built a new stadium.

After three years without the Browns, Cleveland was back on the field in 1999. The team was put together through an expansion draft. But it was not considered an expansion team. To help jump-start the new roster, the Browns had the top pick in the 1999 draft. They used it to select Kentucky's Tim Couch, who was considered the best quarterback prospect.

Fireworks go off inside Cleveland Stadium before the Browns' first game of the 1999 NFL season.

RETAKING THE FIELD

The Browns officially returned to play on September 12, 1999. However, they did so with a crushing loss. Facing one of their historic rivals, the Pittsburgh Steelers, the Browns fell 43–0. That was the start of a seven-game losing streak.

The Browns finally picked up their first win of the season in dramatic fashion. Playing on the road against the New Orleans Saints in Week 8, the Browns trailed 16–14 with two seconds to play. From his own 44, Couch tossed a Hail Mary to the end zone. Two Saints defenders tipped it, and Cleveland wide receiver Kevin Johnson hauled it in. The win was incredible, but victories were rare for the Browns. In their first two seasons back in the NFL, Cleveland won only five games. Couch struggled, and he was frequently hurt.

Quarterback Kelly Holcomb throws a pass against the Pittsburgh Steelers in the playoffs after the 2002 season.

In 2001, Butch Davis became Cleveland's head coach. He briefly turned things around for the team. In his second season, Davis coaxed a decent performance out of Couch, leading the Browns to a 9–7 finish. That was good enough for a wild-card playoff spot. However, the team had to play without Couch, as he had suffered a broken leg late in the season.

The playoff game was in Pittsburgh, and Cleveland backup quarterback Kelly Holcomb played brilliantly. He ended the game with 429 passing yards. Early in the third quarter, his 15-yard touchdown pass to receiver Dennis Northcutt put the Browns up 24–7.

Cleveland led 33–21 with 5:30 left in the game. But the Steelers drove 77 yards to score in just over two minutes. After Cleveland couldn't move the ball on its next drive, the Steelers took over and scored again, adding a two-point conversion for a 36–33 lead. Holcomb desperately drove Cleveland into Pittsburgh territory for a potential game-tying field goal, but time ran out for the Browns at the Steelers' 29-yard line.

STEADY DECLINE

Fans in Cleveland hoped the 2002 season would lead to greater things. Instead, the Browns flopped. Holcomb struggled through a 5–11 season, and Couch was let go the following year. Both Holcomb and Davis had lost their jobs midway through 2004.

That started a pattern for the Browns. The team churned through quarterbacks for several straight losing seasons. Cleveland's only winning record for the rest of the decade was in 2007. The Browns finished 10-6, which was the same record as division-rival Pittsburgh. However, the Steelers were crowned division champions after beating Cleveland in both regular-season meetings. The rest of the AFC was so competitive that the Browns missed the playoffs. The next season, they lost 12 games.

One of the biggest reasons for Cleveland's struggles was poor drafting. Beginning with Couch, the new Browns consistently picked the wrong players in the first round. The 2007 draft was one notable exception. With the No. 3 pick, the Browns picked left tackle Joe Thomas. For the next 11 years, Thomas was a bright light on a losing franchise. Thomas didn't miss a single offensive snap until his final season in 2017, when a triceps injury sidelined him. That was a streak of 10,363 consecutive plays.

"That number 10,363 is special to me—and not just because it's an NFL record, but because it shows that I was there for my brothers 10,363 times in a row," Thomas said. "Loyalty, consistency, something bigger than yourself, showing up for someone else."

In 2023, Thomas was inducted into the Pro Football Hall of Fame. He was the first Browns draft pick to earn that honor since Ozzie Newsome.

Derek Anderson was a surprise star for the 2007 Browns. The quarterback threw for 3,787 yards and 29 touchdowns.

"THAT NUMBER 10,363 IS SPECIAL TO ME . . . BECAUSE IT SHOWS THAT I WAS THERE FOR MY BROTHERS 10,363 TIMES IN A ROW."

—JOE THOMAS

Left tackle Joe Thomas was only the fifth player to reach the Pro Bowl in each of his first 10 seasons in the NFL.

However, even with Thomas's elite skills, the Browns couldn't find the winning spark they needed.

UP FROM THE BOTTOM

Thomas never played on another winning team after his rookie season. And his final year in the NFL was dreadful. The Browns came into the 2017 season having finished just 1–15 the year before, with their only win coming in the second-to-last week of the season. Only one team, the 2008 Detroit Lions, had ever finished winless in a 16-game season.

In 2017, the Browns did everything wrong. The offense scored a league-worst 234 points. Starting quarterback DeShone Kizer, a 21-year-old rookie, threw a league-high 22 interceptions and only 11 touchdowns. The defense wasn't much better. The Browns allowed 410 points, which was fewer than only one other team. Cleveland lost six games by a touchdown or less, including two in overtime. On the final day of the season, the 0–15 Browns lost 28–24 in

A CELEBRATION

Teams usually hold victory parades after championships. In January 2018, Browns fan Chris McNeil held a "Perfect Season" parade to mock the team's 0-16 record during the 2017 season. McNeil gathered fans at the team's home stadium, where they made one lap around the facility. The lap represented the number zero for how many games the team won.

Pittsburgh, sealing Cleveland's fate alongside the 2008 Lions as one of the worst NFL teams in history.

Although the Browns had hit rock bottom, there were promising signs ahead. Rookie defensive end Myles Garrett had seven sacks for the 2017 team. He broke out the next year with 13 1/2 sacks. The Browns slowly surrounded Garrett with more talent. The Browns added standout cornerback Denzel Ward and star runner Nick Chubb in the 2018 NFL Draft. That year, they also picked quarterback Baker Mayfield first overall. In 2018, he set a rookie record for touchdown passes with 27.

By 2020, the Browns were a winning team again. After an 11–5 record under new head coach Kevin Stefanski, the team traveled to Pittsburgh for a wild-card playoff game. The Steelers had been on the other end of many of Cleveland's worst moments since rejoining the league in 1999. But this time, the Browns grabbed a small piece of revenge. Mayfield threw three touchdown passes. Cleveland intercepted Steelers quarterback Ben Roethlisberger four times.

Cornerback Denzel Ward reached the Pro Bowl in three of his first six seasons.

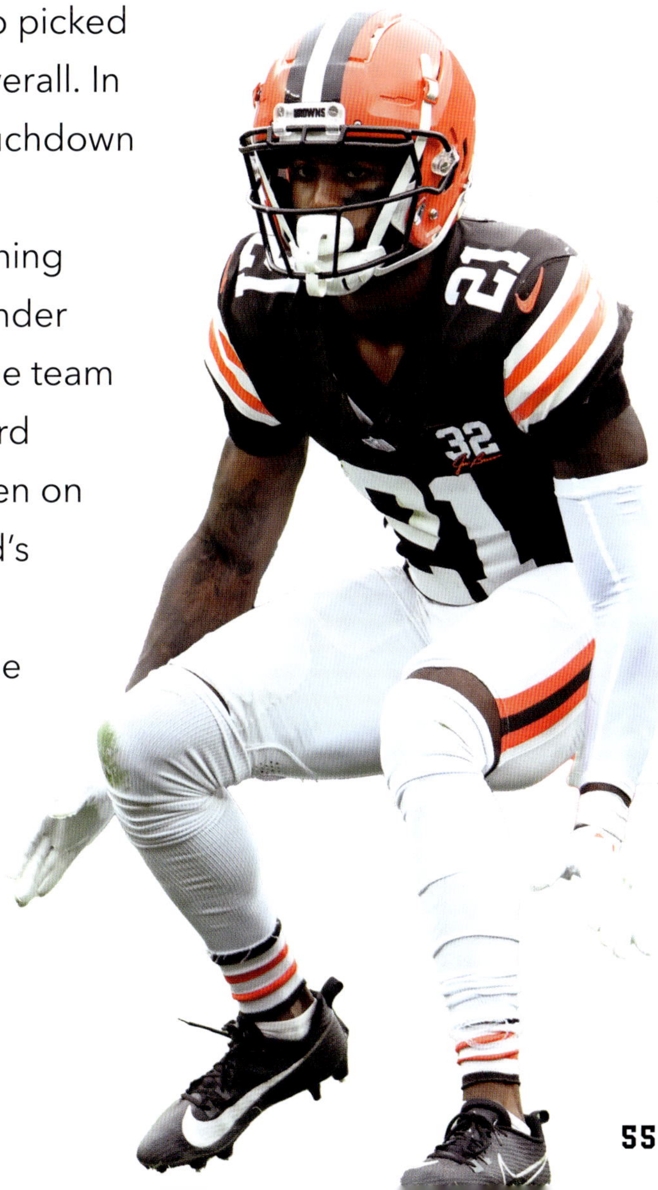

Myles Garrett, *right*, tackles Kansas City Chiefs quarterback Patrick Mahomes during the divisional round of the playoffs after the 2020 season.

The Browns opened up a 35–7 lead, then held on for their first playoff victory since 1994.

The win set up a matchup with the defending Super Bowl champion Kansas City Chiefs in the divisional round. Once again playing on the road, the Browns rallied from a 19–3 deficit, eventually closing the gap to 22–17 early in the fourth quarter. However, the team fell just short.

The success of the 2020 season was short-lived. Mayfield struggled and was eventually traded. Chubb suffered a serious

Quarterback Baker Mayfield electrified Cleveland fans with his play during his first three seasons.

BROWNS TROPHY CASE

SUPER BOWL CHAMPIONSHIPS: 0

AAFC CHAMPIONSHIPS: 4

1946, 1947, 1948, 1949

NFL CHAMPIONSHIPS: 4

1950, 1954, 1955, 1964

DIVISION TITLES: 22

AAFC West: 1946, 1947, 1948, 1949
NFL American: 1950, 1951, 1952
NFL East: 1953, 1954, 1955, 1957, 1958, 1964, 1965
NFL Century: 1967, 1968, 1969
AFC Central: 1971, 1980, 1985, 1986, 1987, 1989

All stats are through the 2024 season.

During the 2024 season, running back Nick Chubb, *right*, passed Mike Pruitt to secure the third most rushing yards in Cleveland's history.

injury early in the 2023 season. But the Browns' tenacious defense, led by Garrett and Ward, got them back to the playoffs. Garrett's performance earned him the NFL's Defensive Player of the Year Award, making him the first Browns player to ever win it. Although the season ended with a wild-card loss to the Houston Texans, Cleveland fans were finally optimistic.

By the start of the 2024 season, the Browns had gone through 12 head coaches since 1999. The team had also used 38 starting quarterbacks. However, Stefanski reached his fifth season in 2024, making him the longest-lasting coach of the team's new era. During that season, the Browns started four different quarterbacks who all struggled to win games, leading to a 3–14 record. While the search for a franchise quarterback continued, the team stuck by Stefanski, confident he could lead Cleveland back to the playoffs.

TIMELINE

1946
The Browns begin play in the AAFC and win the league championship under head coach and minority owner Paul Brown.

Cleveland joins the NFL and wins its first league title.
1950

Cleveland wins the second of back-to-back titles in legendary quarterback Otto Graham's final game.
1955

1957
The Browns draft Jim Brown, who goes on to set NFL records for rushing yards and touchdowns.

Advertising executive Art Modell purchases the Browns.
1961

1962
Modell controversially fires Paul Brown.

For the second year in a row, the Browns lose the NFL Championship Game and miss out on the newly created Super Bowl.
1969

1981
"The Kardiac Kids" reach the divisional round but lose to the Oakland Raiders 14–12 on January 4.

1988
Earnest Byner's fumble costs the Browns a chance to tie the AFC title game against the Denver Broncos on January 17.

1995
Modell announces he is moving the Browns to Baltimore, prompting protest in Cleveland.

1999
After an agreement with the NFL, the Browns resume play in Cleveland.

2007
Left tackle Joe Thomas is drafted by the Browns.

2017
Cleveland becomes the second team to finish a 16-game NFL season without a win.

2021
The Browns return to the playoffs for the first time in 18 years, but they fall to the Kansas City Chiefs in the divisional round on January 17.

2023
Myles Garrett wins the NFL's Defensive Player of the Year Award.

GLOSSARY

civil rights–the freedoms and liberties guaranteed to individuals by the government.

draft–a system that allows teams to acquire new players coming into a league.

expansion draft–a special draft held to stock a new team using players from existing teams in the same league.

expansion team–a new team that is added to an existing league.

franchise–an entire sports organization.

general manager–an executive who runs a team and is responsible for finding and signing players.

Hail Mary–a long pass that has a small chance of succeeding, usually made near the end of a game as a last-ditch effort to score.

iconic–well known for excellence.

infamous–well known for negative reasons.

legacy–something of importance that came from someone in the past.

merge–join with another to create something new, such as a company, a team, or a league.

Pro Bowl–a postseason competition that the NFL's all-stars are invited to compete in.

rival–an opponent with whom a player or team has a fierce and ongoing competition.

rookie–a professional athlete in his or her first year of competition.

sack–a tackle of the quarterback behind the line of scrimmage before he can pass the ball.

safety—a score of two points for a team when its opponent is unable to advance the ball out of its own end zone.

scout—a person whose job is to look for talented young players.

segregate—to separate groups of people based on race, gender, ethnicity, or other factors.

two-point conversion—an option for teams that have scored a touchdown to try a running or passing play from the two-yard line for two points, instead of kicking for one point.

veteran—someone who has played for many years.

ONLINE RESOURCES

Booklinks
NONFICTION NETWORK
FREE! ONLINE NONFICTION RESOURCES

To learn more about Cleveland Browns, please visit **abdobooklinks.com** or scan this QR code. These links are routinely monitored and updated to provide the most current information available.

INDEX